Althea Gibson

Althea Gibson

a i Academic Industries, Inc.
West Haven, Connecticut 06516

ISBN 0-88301-795-4

Published by
Academic Industries, Inc.
The Academic Building
Saw Mill Road
West Haven, Connecticut 06516

Printed in the United States of America

Althea Gibson

Contents

Althea Gibson always wanted to be somebody important.

It was not easy for her to grow up in a ghetto.   It was not easy to be a world tennis champion   either. But Althea did both. This is her story.

Growing Up
in the Ghetto

Althea Gibson was born on a farm in South Carolina in 1927.

I know you wanted a boy, Daniel.

Well, Annie, this little one looks like she's got as much fight in her as any man.

Althea's father was a poor cotton farmer.

The crop looks bad, Annie. I just don't know how much longer we can make it down here.

For three years, the cotton crop had been poor. Sometimes, Daniel and Annie Gibson had to live on only seventy-five dollars a year.

I'm worried. I think we'll have to move to the city so I can find work.

I know how much you love this farm, but the children must have food.

When Althea was three, her Aunt Sally came to visit.

Sally, I just can't make a living on this farm anymore. We'll be moving north.

Why don't you let me take little Althea with me now? You can pack and come later.

Althea and her aunt took the train to New York.

Soon Althea's father joined them.

I got a job that pays ten dollars a week! I'll be able to send for your Mama real soon.

Finally the whole Gibson family had moved to New York City.

They lived in Harlem.   Life was different than in South Carolina.

Oh, Daniel! I'm afraid those boys are going to beat up our Althea.

But Althea learned city ways quickly. She could take care of herself.

Oh, no! I'm afraid she's going to beat *them* up!

Young Althea loved to play street games.

Althea! I'm tired of calling you. Come in for dinner right now!

Just one more game— please?

But most of all she loved movies.

Wow, I could see that again!

We can do that and still be home in time for dinner.

She loved stage shows at the Apollo Theater.

Singing like that just makes me want to cry!

In fact, Althea loved street games, the Apollo Theater, and movies much more than school.

That's right, she hasn't been to school for over a month, Mr. Gibson.

Well, she'll get a good spanking for this!

And so she did.

I don't like doing this, but someone has got to knock some sense into you.

Her father was right. Yet Althea wouldn't listen. She went to school, but not to learn.

Althea became wilder and wilder. Sometimes she slept on subway trains.

Boy, I hate coming here. It's a good place to meet, though. Let's go to the movies.

We did that yesterday. Let's go bowling today.

Hey, little girl, wake up.

POCKET BIOGRAPHIES

Mrs. Gibson, this is Officer O'Malley. Your daughter is down here at the police station.

Child, I just don't know what's to become of you!

Somehow Althea finished junior high school. Then, she went to work. Her work record was not much better than her school record had been.

This is a terrible job. I quit!

The
First Taste
of Tennis

After quitting her job, Althea spent most of her time with her friends. She also played on a girls' basketball team.

Good game, girls. You're the hottest team in the league.

We know!

Come on, gang. Let's go bowling.

One night Althea met Sugar Ray Robinson, the great boxer.

Althea, this is Sugar Ray Robinson.

So you're Sugar Ray. Well, I can beat you in bowling!

Sugar Ray and his wife, Edna Mae, liked Althea right away.

Hey kid, you'd better sleep here tonight. We don't want you sleeping in the subway.

Meanwhile, the police made 143rd Street, where Althea's parents lived, into a play street. They closed it to cars so that children could play paddleball there. Althea was very good at it.

Buddy Walker was one of the play leaders during the summer. He liked the way Althea hit the ball.

Here, Althea. I want you to try hitting the ball with this tennis racket.

Soon Althea could make a tennis ball go in any direction she wanted.

Great shot, kid! I want you to come to the Harlem River Tennis Club with me on Saturday.

Okay, but you have to buy me lunch.

I'll be happy to help her with her game.

Buddy's friends' arranged for Althea to join a fancy tennis club. They also paid for her lessons.

Match to Miss Gibson!

So you're Fred Johnson—the one-armed pro.

That's right, Althea. I'm going to teach you some of the finer points of this game.

Althea learned quickly. At this time, however, black people were not allowed to play in the American Lawn Tennis Association matches. So Althea played in matches held by another group, and she became the New York City champion.

23

Meanwhile, she still spent time with Sugar Ray and Edna Mae. Sugar Ray had a set of drums. Althea loved to hear him play.

Edna Mae, do you think Sugar Ray would buy me a saxophone so I could play, too?

Well, honey, the only way to find out is to ask.

Sugar Ray agreed, and gave Althea the money to buy her saxophone.

Oh boy, thanks for coming along to help me.

I'm glad to. But don't let this hurt your tennis game.

PAWN SHOP

Althea's saxophone squeaked and screamed. But still she loved to play.

In 1946, Althea played in the American Tennis Association's women's singles championship.

She lost the match, but she had played very well. Sugar Ray waited for her afterward.

Dr. Eaton invited Althea to move to Wilmington, North Carolina. There she could live with his family and play tennis while she went to high school.

Althea, I want you to meet Dr. Eaton and Dr. Johnson. They think you could be a great tennis player.

Sugar Ray, do you think I should do it?

You'll never amount to anything if you keep on like you've been doing. No matter what you want to do, you'll be better at it if you go to school first.

So in September, Althea took the train ticket Dr. Eaton sent her and headed south.

GRAND CENTRAL ST

25

Dr. Eaton was rich. This was a new and different life for Althea. But his family made her feel at home.

It's wonderful to be here.

Althea, we're glad to have you with us.

For the first time in her life, Althea worked hard in school. And she played in the band.

But she worked even harder after school on the tennis court behind Dr. Eaton's home.

Good shot, Althea. You're getting too good for me already.

Tournament Play

For the next three years Althea lived with the Eatons. She went to school and played tennis with Dr. Eaton. He loved to watch her beat his friends.

This young lady is too good for me!

It's all Dr. Eaton's doing.

In the summers, Dr. Johnson drove Althea, his son, and other young people around the country to play in tennis tournaments.

She's worked hard this year. Now she needs to face some good players.

I'll see to that!

In 1947, Althea played again in the American Tennis Association's women's singles championship. This time she didn't lose.

She won again the following year, and for the third time in 1949. Her teachers thought she was ready for bigger things.

We want to have a good black tennis player take part in the important "white" tournaments. Do you want to give it a try?

You bet I do!

Many good things are happening to our people in this century. You can help open an important door that's been closed to black people for a long time.

If I *can* do it, it's only because a lot of fine folks have helped me.

That summer she was accepted into two USLTA tournaments. She didn't win, but she showed herself to be a good player.

Finally Althea finished high school. And in September, 1950, she began college. She had won an athletic scholarship.

The next summer Althea got her big break. The Orange Lawn Tennis Club in Orange, New Jersey let her play in the Eastern Grass Court Championships. At last she was being given a chance to prove herself.

Although she lost, she played well. Then later that summer, she received some exciting news.

It's from the president of the American Lawn Tennis Association. He says I can play at Forest Hills!

The Forest Hills tournament in New York was the most important tournament in the United States. No black person had ever before been allowed to play in it.

It was an exciting morning for Althea when she took the subway to Forest Hills.

In her first match she played against Barbara Knapp from England.

She won easily. She would now play in the semi-finals.

The next day she played Louise Brough, once the champion of the United States.

Louise was a very good player. She took an early lead over Althea.

But Althea came back to even the score.

The match was very close. Suddenly it began to rain. The game had to be stopped for the day.

If it hadn't rained, perhaps Althea might have won. But the next day she was far from calm. She lost in a close match.

Few people become stars overnight. Althea had made a good start, but she had many years of hard work ahead before she would get to the top.

In 1952, Althea was ranked number nine of all women tennis players in the U.S. In 1953, she moved up to number seven. But in 1954, she dropped to number thirteen. She was very unhappy.

That same year she finished college.

Congratulations.

She got a job teaching sports at Lincoln University in Missouri. At that time, black people were still not allowed to sit with white people in some places.

COLORED

As a child, Althea had liked sitting in the balcony at the movies. But she hated being made to sit there just because she was black.

Althea had a friend who was in the army. There, he told her, things were different.

Why don't you join the army? You'll make good money, and people will treat you well.

You're right. I'm getting nowhere with tennis. I'll do it.

So in 1955, when the school year was over, Althea drove back to Harlem. She spoke of her new plans to Sidney Llewellyn, a Harlem tennis teacher who was one of Althea's closest friends.

But you can do that if you stick to tennis.

You think so, and maybe I think so— but we're the only ones. No, I'm finished in tennis.

But you've got a great future in tennis!

If I were really any good I'd be champion by now. I'm sick of having other people give me money. I want to take care of myself.

But just before she joined the army, a wonderful thing happened. Althea was playing at Forest Hills one day.

Renville McMann. I work for the government. How would you like to go with the U.S. Tennis Team to Asia?

Are you kidding? I'd love to!

And so Althea went with three other Americans to spread good will. Once again, tennis had changed her life.

This is wonderful!

The U.S. team played tennis in places like Dacca, Pakistan. They saw many strange and exciting things.

Althea decided that the tennis life wasn't so bad after all!

Winning
at
Wimbledon
and
Forest Hills

On her way home from Asia, Althea won the French National Championships. She was the first black person to win a major tournament in a country besides the U.S.

So this is Paris!

The most important tennis tournament in the world is held in England. In 1956, Althea played in the championship at Wimbledon —against another American, Shirley Fry. She lost.

Of course I'm sorry I lost. But I played well. Soon I'll be the best in the world.

She was right. Althea's year was 1957. When she finally won at Wimbledon, Queen Elizabeth herself was there to give her the trophy.

Congratulations.

Thank you very much.

Messages of congratulation came from many people, even from President Eisenhower. In New York, a newspaperman talked to Althea's father.

She wanted to try for the top, and she finally made it. I knew she was strong enough to do it.

What do you mean?

Well, she had to go through so much and work so hard. I'm proud of her.

When Althea returned to New York, the city welcomed her home with a parade.

The mayor gave her a medal from the city.

You have shown that somewhere in the great American dream, there is a place for black people as well as white.

And that fall, Althea finally won the U.S. championship at Forest Hills. Vice president Richard Nixon gave her the prize.

It was wonderful to win at Wimbledon. But it's even better to be the champion of my own country!

Althea Gibson had many interests:

going to movies

singing

playing tennis

playing saxophone

playing golf

She knew she had to succeed at one of them. She wanted to prove to herself and to the world that she was "somebody."

Tennis gave her this chance. She learned what she needed to do to become the best—and then she did it.

THE END

Do you remember?

Althea was born on a quiet farm in South Carolina. When she was three, her aunt took her to:

a. Kentucky.   b. New York.   c. California.

Althea moved to North Carolina so she could work on her:

a. tennis.   b. horseback riding.   c. saxophone.

Althea was the first black person invited to play in:

a. the Forest Hills tournament.
b. Orange Lawn Tennis Club.
c. Carnegie Hall.

The World Championship of tennis is played at:

a. Forest Hills, New York.
b. Paris, France.
c. Wimbledon, England.

Quiz
Yourself

Words to know

champion	a person who wins first place in a game or contest
ghetto	part of a city where people of the same background live
semi-finals	a match to see who will play in the championship
subway	trains that run on underground tracks
future	a time to come

Can you use them?

Using the words above, complete the following sentences.

1. Althea's family lived in a _____ in New York.

2. In large cities, people can get from one place to another by riding the _____ .

3. Thanks to Althea, the _____ for black athletes was more promising.

4. The tennis players who win the _____ will play one another in the finals to see who is champion.

5. When Althea was thirty years old, she became a world tennis _____ .

Using pictures

In reading illustrated stories, you will find it helpful to "read" the pictures as well as the words. Look at this picture of the Gibsons' home in South Carolina. It shows us that the Gibsons were poor. They used a lantern for light because they had no electricity.  Mrs. Gibson had to cook the meals on the potbellied stove which also heated their small home. Look carefully at the other pictures as you read, and you will learn more about Althea's life.

While you are reading

If you had known Althea when she was a young girl, you would never have guessed she'd become a famous sportswoman.

While you are reading, make a list of all the things that happened to Althea which changed her life and helped her become a famous tennis player.

_____

_____

_____

_____

_____

_____

How well did you read?

When you have finished reading, answer the following questions.

1.   When did Althea first begin playing tennis?

(Check the correct answer.)

_____ a.   when she was in junior high school

_____ b.   just before she moved to New York

_____ c.   when the street she lived on was made into a play street

_____ d.   after Sugar Ray Robinson beat her in bowling

2.   Which of the following were refused to Althea because she was black?

(Check the correct *answers.*)

_____ a.   sitting with white people in some places

_____ b.   sleeping in the subway trains

_____ c.   "cutting" school to go to the movies

_____ d.   playing in certain tennis tournaments

POCKET BIOGRAPHIES

3. At one point in her life, Althea stopped playing tennis because:

    (Check the correct *answers.*)

    _____ a.   the United States
                 government offered
                 her a job.

    _____ b.   she wanted to earn
                 her own money.

    _____ c.   she planned to marry
                 Fred Johnson, the
                 tennis pro.

    _____ d.   she didn't believe
                 she was good enough
                 to be a tennis player.

4. Which of the following people helped Althea during her struggle to become "somebody"?

    (Check the correct *answers.*)

    _____ a.   Buddy Walker, who gave
                 Althea her first tennis
                 racket

    _____ b.   Barbara Knapp, who in-
                 vited Althea to England

    _____ c.   her father, who insisted
                 that Althea go to school

    _____ d.   her Aunt Sally, who paid
                 for Althea's schooling

    _____ e.   Fred Johnson, who gave Althea tennis lessons

    _____ f.   Queen Elizabeth, who gave Althea a trophy

    _____ g.   Renville McMann, who kept Althea from joining
                 the army

50

5. Besides tennis, Althea had many other interests. She liked:

(Check the correct *answers.*)

_____ a.   fishing.

_____ b.   seeing movies.

_____ c.   playing the saxophone.

_____ d.   horseback riding.

_____ e.   going dancing.

_____ f.   playing golf.

Using what you've read

Althea was often in the newspapers, not only because she was such a good tennis player, but because she was the first black to play in many tournaments. What do you think the papers said about her? Write a short newspaper article to go with the headline below:

First Black Woman Wins
Tennis Tournament at Wimbledon

Remember, a newspaper article always tells *WHO* is involved, *WHAT* happened, *WHERE* it happened, *WHEN* it happened, and *WHY* it happened.

ALTHEA GIBSON

Can you use them?

1. ghetto
2. subway
3. future
4. semi-finals

5. champion

How well did you read?

1. c
2. a, d
3. b, d
4. a, c, e, g

5. b, c, e, f

NOTES

NOTES

NOTES

COMPLETE LIST OF POCKET CLASSICS AVAILABLE

CLASSICS

C 1 Black Beauty
C 2 The Call of the Wild
C 3 Dr. Jekyll and Mr. Hyde
C 4 Dracula
C 5 Frankenstein
C 6 Huckleberry Finn
C 7 Moby Dick
C 8 The Red Badge of Courage
C 9 The Time Machine
C10 Tom Sawyer
C11 Treasure Island
C12 20,000 Leagues Under the Sea
C13 The Great Adventures of Sherlock Holmes
C14 Gulliver's Travels
C15 The Hunchback of Notre Dame
C16 The Invisible Man
C17 Journey to the Center of the Earth
C18 Kidnapped
C19 The Mysterious Island
C20 The Scarlet Letter
C21 The Story of My Life
C22 A Tale of Two Cities
C23 The Three Musketeers
C24 The War of the Worlds
C25 Around the World in Eighty Days
C26 Captains Courageous
C27 A Connecticut Yankee in King Arthur's Court
C28 The Hound of the Baskervilles
C29 The House of the Seven Gables
C30 Jane Eyre

COMPLETE LIST OF POCKET CLASSICS AVAILABLE
(cont'd)

COMPLETE LIST OF POCKET CLASSICS AVAILABLE
(cont'd)

SHAKESPEARE

COMPLETE LIST OF POCKET CLASSICS AVAILABLE

BIOGRAPHIES

B 1 Charles Lindbergh
B 2 Amelia Earhart
B 3 Houdini
B 4 Walt Disney
B 5 Davy Crockett
B 6 Daniel Boone
B 7 Elvis Presley
B 8 The Beatles
B 9 Benjamin Franklin
B10 Martin Luther King, Jr.
B11 Abraham Lincoln
B12 Franklin D. Roosevelt
B13 George Washington
B14 Thomas Jefferson
B15 Madame Curie
B16 Albert Einstein
B17 Thomas Edison
B18 Alexander Graham Bell
B19 Vince Lombardi
B20 Pelé
B21 Babe Ruth
B22 Jackie Robinson
B23 Jim Thorpe
B24 Althea Gibson